In the Enchanted Garden

Words by Norman C. Habel
Pictures by Jim Roberts

Concordia Publishing House

A PURPLE PUZZLE TREE BOOK

Would you like to take a trip with me
to an old enchanted garden?
Would you like to take a walk with me
down the garden paths of Eden?
Would you like to see what Adam saw
in that bright enchanted garden?

Then follow me!
We're off to see
a garden full of fun,
with special joys
for girls and boys
and thrills for everyone.

The first surprise
when you open your eyes
is Adam and Eve together.
They have no clothes
from head to toes,
for it's always sunny weather.

But they don't feel naked
and they don't feel naughty,
the way we do so many times.
Everyone is happy here
and everything is bright.
The animals are laughing,
laughing with delight.

Look!
Over there on the garden seat!
It's a long green candy cane.
It looks so pretty and so sweet.
Oh, no it's not!
It's a long green snake
standing on its tail.
He's beckoning for us to come.
He wants to be our guide, I think,
along the garden trail.
Adam and Eve are following him
along the enchanted track.

Don't you want to come with me?
Only cowards ever turn back!

We're going to the enchanted forest
deep in the enchanted garden,
where many trees have magic fruit
and bushes have magic berries.

Look! Can you see?
That tree there is a color tree,
and the berries look like lights.
If you eat that fruit with me,
you can change your color
from brown to blue,
or yellow, red, or white,
if that's what pleases you!
Well, does it?

Look! Can you see?
That tall tree is a growing-up tree
with beans like on a beanstalk.
And if you eat those beans with me,
you can grow to seven feet two,
and you can be a giant,
if that's what pleases you.
Well, does it?

Look! Can you see?
That green tree is a long-life tree.
Its nuts are very hard.
But if you eat those nuts with me,
you can live like angels do
and never, never die,

if that's what pleases you.
Well, does it?

Look! Can you see?
Over there is another tree
that's very dark and strange.
They say it's called the learning tree,
but that's a magic name.
I wonder what will happen
if we eat its bright red fruit?
The fruit just looks like candy cane.
It must taste very sweet.
Well, now, are you game?
Quick, take some now
before God sees us coming.

Wait!
Look! Look over there!
The snake and Eve have stopped
beside the learning tree.
The snake is asking Eve a question.
Do you want to listen in
and hear just what they say?

"Do you mean to tell me," asks the snake,
"God really said:
'You cannot eat of any fruit
in this enchanted garden?'"

Eve replied, "You're wrong! You're wrong!
God said that we could eat
from any tree we wished
in this enchanted garden.

But we cannot eat
from the learning tree,
or touch its bright red fruit,
or otherwise we'll die."

The snake just made a dirty grin
and whispered in Eve's ear,
"God knows as well as you and I
you won't really die, my dear.
For if you eat the bright red fruit
from the magic learning tree,
you'll know as much as God knows!
Your eyes will pop wide open
and you'll learn an old, old secret
of just why God is God!"

There was magic in the air!
There was magic everywhere!
Eve wanted that fruit so much!
And what was wrong with a little touch?
Well, what was?

So she touched it. Wouldn't you?
And she took it. Wouldn't you?
And she tasted it. Wouldn't you?
And she ate it! Wouldn't you?
And she gave some to Adam,
and to me, and you and you.
And then...
And then...
And then...
Suddenly!
Their eyes popped open wide
just like yours and mine.
For the first time in their life
they learned so many things.
They learned that they were naked.
And they learned that they were naughty,
just the way we do,
when we steal or disobey.
They learned that they were scared,
and they learned that they might die
if God could ever find them
hiding in the garden.

Quiet!
Listen! Can you hear?
It sounds like God is coming,
walking slowly through the garden.
He's looking for His Adam and Eve.
"Adam," said God, "Where are you?
Why are you hiding from Me?
Did you do something wrong?
Did you steal from that tree?
Well, did you, Adam, did you?"

"She started it all," said Adam to God.
"She's really a very bad girl!"
"I didn't! I didn't!" cried Eve.
"That sassy green snake over there.
He started it all! Don't blame it on me!
He told me a lie about that strange
learning tree.
He tricked me. He tricked me.
It just isn't fair!"

Then God was sad and said aloud,
"I'll have to punish you all
for spoiling the world I made.
Now the spell is broken
and all the world is cracked.
The world is like a puzzle now,
with pieces out of place.
The animals aren't laughing
and people hate each other.
So I will have to find a way
to put this puzzle back together."

Look! Look again!
Adam and Eve are very, very sad.
They know they've been naughty.
But God still loves them both.
He's giving them a birthday present.
He is giving them some brand-new clothes,
two lovely purple gowns.
Now they won't feel naked.
And perhaps they won't feel naughty
anymore!

The enchanted garden disappeared
and the magic trees all vanished.
Then God was gone and all was gone,
all except their purple gowns.
For the gowns were like two precious parts
of a mixed-up purple puzzle.

Now if we want to know God's plan
for this great big mixed-up world.
Well, we must find the puzzle parts
and learn just how
God is putting them back together.

the PURPLE PUZZLE TREE